The NEW REAL ESTATE

"10 SECRETS that will put MONEY in YOUR POCKET!" (Even though, up until now, houses only COST you money.)

DON MARTIN

Copyright © 2014 Don Martin

All rights reserved.

ISBN: 1494983109
ISBN-13: 978-1494983109

DEDICATION

This book is dedicated to my family and my best friend, Riley. They have always been patient with me.

CONTENTS

Foreword i

1 Exposure 1

2 MLS 5

3 Pictures 15

4 Tent Signs 22

5 Points 25

6 Buyer Incentives 31

7 Agent Incentive 35

8 QR Codes 39

9 Seller Help 42

10 Agent Help 47

The NEW REAL ESTATE
FOREWARD

I can almost see you right now as you are thinking about reading this book. That's how clearly I picture you. It is time for you to change your address, maybe buy a new house and sell an old one. Address-changers fall into two categories- those who spent a lot more money than they had to in the process but don't mind (or realized too late), and those who suspect there is a better, less expensive way to do this. I can't help the first group, but in the second group there are some questions, some fears and some doubts because the property transaction process is not at all intuitive. Those people I can help. Those problems I can ease. After thirty years of doing this, maybe I have seen something that will help you. I won't give everybody a fish. But I will teach you how to fish. And where to look for the fish.

Several times and in a lot of places you will hear that some topics are beyond the scope of this book. This book is intended to be a broad over-view of a new mind-set, a new way of doing real estate. It is not intended to be a how-to course for either sellers, buyers or agents. Those will come in subsequent books.

Some of these secrets will save you money, some of these secrets will make you money, some will save you time trying to sell or buy. And don't forget time is money. Every once in a while, the sale of a house will let you successfully buy the new one you're in love with or escape some unpleasant destiny. In those circumstances, time is a lot more than money!

In 1986 a movie was released starring Tom Hanks and Shelley Long, entitled *The Money Pit*, where a couple purchased a house and tried to renovate it. To one degree or another, all of us who have owned a house have felt this way about it. In some ways it is like the boat owner's story that the two happiest days in the life of a boat owner are the day that he buys it and the day that he sells it.

Houses have cost us to buy, to keep, to maintain, to fix up and improve, and finally, they cost us a bundle to sell. But it doesn't have to be that way. This book will start to describe to you a way to actually end up further over on the plus side of the ledger when you sell or buy a house. Some of these concepts will be totally new to you, some will be just a fresh perspective on an older idea. We have been assembling these for the better part of three decades.

Remember, as a seller, it is your job to sell your house quickly and get every dime out of it that you can for a change. And as a buyer, it is your job to keep every dime you can in your pocket or, if possible, put some more dimes

The NEW REAL ESTATE
in it!

In some of our other books and workshops we will more deeply address the processes of these concepts as they apply to real estate agents and to people who are selling their own houses. This is an introductory course, The New Real Estate 101.

I will touch on some financing issues for sellers and buyers, some presentation issues for sellers and some representation issues for buyers and sellers. My background is as a thirty-year agent/broker who has expanded from traditional representation of buyers and sellers to a more relaxed representation of both. In my world, you, the consumer, has the choice of being more involved and "hands-on" in the transactions, resulting in huge money savings.

My Graduated Services Real Estate approach is not for everyone, and is no more a "one-size-fits-all" method than the traditional methods. You get to choose what feels best for you. The important thing to know is that you have these choices. Try one or two, or all of them- it's up to you. None of these choices have to involve me, but they should involve you. The greater your knowledge and participation, the better off you are.

DON MARTIN

The NEW REAL ESTATE

1 EXPOSURE

(MONEY SECRET #1 - FOR SELLERS)

There are some people who need to sell their house. It could be summer. It could be winter. It could be pleasant weather, or not. It could even be Christmas. Maybe they are being transferred and need to move to a different city. Maybe they are going to have a baby or some other addition to their family. Maybe they just lost their job or some of their overtime and they just can't keep on at whatever level they were. They all just want to sell their house and move.

Here is the first concept. Secret number one (this one for sellers) is a double-barreled one. Let people know it is for sale, and then, get out of the way. That's really all there is to it. Out there, somewhere is the perfect person for your house. They just don't know it's for sale yet. So let a lot of people know until you get to the right person. Then get out of the way. Your house will sell itself, if you let it and the buyer will buy it, if you let them.

So that leads us to two more questions. How do you let enough people know about your house? And how to keep from messing up? Besides that, I have two requirements driving me- I want to get the most out of my house that I possibly can, AND I'm in a kind of a rush. What now?

I want as much as I can get out of it.

Over the last few years we have had some mysterious disappearing equity. Many houses are worth less now, some less than when they were purchased some years ago. Some people walked away their houses. Some did what is called a short sale, where the bank agrees to take less than owed in a sale situation, rather than risk losing even more. Some were just bank foreclosures, and some were sold the plain, old fashioned way.

Most of the time, in fact, in all but the most dire of situations, people are concerned with getting every dollar of their equity out of their house when they sell it.

I am in a hurry to get to the next chapter of my life.

The NEW REAL ESTATE

There are some people who need to sell their house quickly. In many if not most situations people don't really want to move in the beginning. But as time goes on, they get more and more motivated.

The bank won't play ball anymore. The note is eating into my savings every month. After the baby, we are stacked on top of each other. The place is falling apart and I can't afford to keep it up. It costs a fortune to heat/cool this huge place. Sooner or later they are ready to move and quickly is better than slowly at this point.

In days gone by, we could just put a for sale sign in the yard, especially if we lived on a busy street and sell the house fairly soon. Then we also had to put an ad in the newspaper, and maybe have an open house or two.

Now, trying to sell a house like that would take forever. The key to selling a house is exposure. Your next door neighbor might be a buyer for your house, but if he doesn't know it's for sale, it won't do much good.

There is ONE WAY to get your house in front of the maximum number of eyes RAPIDLY... put it in the Multiple Listing Service (MLS).

DON MARTIN

When a home is described in the MLS, information about it becomes available to all the members of the MLS, Realtors, many of whom are working with someone who will be a good match for your home right now.

As important as that, when a house goes in the MLS, many second and third-party websites spider in to gather the information on your house and place it in their own websites, thus multiplying the possibility that your house gets seen by the right person.

So the MLS is FAST. It is immediate and within another few days, the details about your house is available far and wide in places you never realized existed.

The NEW REAL ESTATE

2 MLS

(MONEY SECRET #2 - FOR SELLERS)

There are two ways to get your house in the MLS. To get information into the MLS, a person must have a real estate license from their state, be a member of the area and National Board of Realtors, and finally, also be a member of the Multiple Listing Service. There are no particularly easy or inexpensive ways to obtain or maintain membership in those three organizations. Consequently, both of the ways involve Realtors.

The architecture of **traditional real estate** involves the listing of a seller's house in return for a commitment by that seller to let the listing Realtor's Brokerage company keep a certain amount of the proceeds of the sale. It usually amounts to a certain percentage of the sale price. This has been going on for years without a real problem. As the price of houses rise, even if the percentages remain the same, the cost of sale has risen fairly sharply.

When high commission is combined with activities of some of the agents, there has built some resentment. This has resulted in an increase of the alternative method of selling a house which is done by the owner directly and not through an agent.

Of course, it is not at all practical even if possible for the homeowner to become a Realtor to sell their house, but they can find Realtors who practice a different architecture model of their industry called flat-rate listing or **limited service listing**. We at Martin Properties have practiced Graduated Services Real Estate for over ten years, in which a seller who can do part of the job of selling their own house can employ us only for the part they cannot do, such as get their house into the MLS.

I. Traditional real estate AGENT - Exclusive Right to Sell

If you call an agent to sell your house, most will come running fairly quickly, and do what it takes to get your house in the MLS as soon as possible. The down side is that they will have you sign a pledge of 6 or 7 percent of the

The NEW REAL ESTATE
selling price for them to list your house.

If you decide to sell your house in this manner, you need to interview a couple of agents before you make a decision. If you have friends who have a recommendation about an agent, by all means include that agent in your interview list but still do the list.

You want to find an agent who has been in the business a number of years and knows what they are doing. There is a lot of knowledge that comes from repetition in the business and it truly is nothing you adequately learn in the licensing process. The real estate business is really pretty easy to get into and easy to get out of, so it's easy to be tentative while you are in it. So you want to try to find an agent who is pretty devoted to doing an excellent job.

Who ever you choose, it is probably a good thing to let them know what you would like for them to do. People are more likely to do what you inspect than what you expect, so let them know up front what a perfect agent would do in your world.

Tell them your thoughts about keeping the listing fresh and ask them how they stay in touch with their sellers. A call every week or two should be reasonable, not too taxing on the agent, and not to invasive to your life as a seller. Just get a check-in about calls and showings. One note- often people think it is a great idea to get "feedback" from agents who have shown the house. But this is not that beneficial. If an agent is pretty good at what they are doing and busy, showing several houses a day much less a week, they don't remember every house and every comment. They will not have much worth hearing. If there is a wall falling down, chances are you already know about it, so you don't need to hear that from the agent.

Actually if an agent is busy working with buyers, it gets aggravating to have to stop and hear from a bunch of listing agents wanting feedback from you. They will probably tell you anything... or nothing. So think about not asking for feedback.

Another thing you might do is look for agents who have several listings in your area. That means he will know the neighborhood and will be showing there anyway. The only trouble is that occasionally, the high volume, high volume agent can get an inflated view of themselves. And sometimes someone with a lower profile might be a better bet on the buy side if you do intend to buy a house.

The perfect agent to help you in a buy side transaction is someone who is not greedy. For an agent to get a transaction out of the blue, that he was not expecting and did not have to work on forever is a blessing to him. You will set up an agreement that you will all but find your own next house and let them do the paperwork in return for sharing that blessing with you.

II. Limited Service – For-Sale-By-Owner (FSBO) - With an Exclusive Agency Agreement

If you don't mind doing some of the work you can sell your house yourself and save a tremendous amount of money. You will still need an agent for this way to sell your house, but it will have to be one with a different background and attitude. In my company we call it Graduated Real Estate Services, but what ever they call it, they need to give you a listing that will be a low flat rate, paid up front. They will need to provide you with the paperwork and be able to edit your listing from time to time when you ask. They will need to keep the MLS current or you will run the risk of having your listing taken out of the MLS. And you have already paid for your listing. That is a waste of money. And we try to keep money from being wasted.

Less commission usually means more profit. When a person signs a commission pledge with an agent, they will usually pledge a percent of the sale price of the house, whether it is five, six, or seven percent. That commission is broken down into two separate parts, some for the "listing agent", the one to whom you pledge the money and whose sign will probably be in your yard, and the other part for the "selling agent," (the other agent if there is another agent,) who is usually working already with the buyer, showing them houses.

Sometimes the listing agent will be working with a buyer who may be interested in your house or at times a buyer just drives by and calls the telephone number of the person on the sign. However it happens, if the house sells under those circumstances, the listing agent would be entitled to both sides of the commission.

Just remember everything is negotiable. In your listing agreement, you have the opportunity to address this possibility, but it is really probably better that you bring it up rather than wait for the agent to do so.

Different situations and different states may refer to this as a facilitator or a disclosed dual agent, but you have the opportunity to agree that the agent would not get the full commission but only a lesser specified portion.

The trick is that an agent may tell someone that they would have to do twice as much work if they are representing both the buyer and seller, but that is not really the case. As a matter of fact, once the actual negotiation is settled on price, when the situation is not adversarial, you could all sit down at the kitchen table, and all work as a team to co-ordinate the various inspections and appraisals.

These listing pledges are usually described as exclusive "Right to Sell" agreements where even if you sell your house yourself, you will be indebted to the listing broker for their commission.

More profit

Remember the public is demanding and a bit fickle. They want what they want and they want it right then. Agents can sometimes be demanding as well. If you have more control over your situation, you may have less demand from agents but more from the public.

Many agents these days are a part of a team and many work with an independent third-party company who sets up showing appointments for other Realtors. A Realtor, wanting to show a property calls a central phone number where someone sets up the showing appointment and gives the Realtor instructions.

Ideally, the seller's house is accessible and maybe on a MLS lock so it's easy to show. Sometimes the showing center has to call the owner/seller and confirm the appointment with them. The trick is that NOBODY in this equation wants the owner to say "no." The request has gone through the layers of bureaucracy so far that you just better say "OK."

If the seller says no, then the requesting agent screams at the showing service. The prospective buyer screams at the requesting agent. The listing agent screams at the owner/seller. Nobody is happy.

Now the listing agent must impress on the owner/seller the importance of accessibility. Sometimes the seller and agent can agree ahead that the house can be shown on Tuesdays and Thursdays between noon and 2pm. Even though that works for the seller and is agreed to by the listing agent, it's hard to get everybody else on board with the plan. Accessibility is the key.

The difficulty is in planning ahead with other parties. If you were selling your house yourself, you could tell the prospective buyer that you were busy at that exact time, but mention an alternative. Even if your house were listed with a Realtor who worked his own listings, you could possibly do that. But when you are working with another member of a Realtor's team or with a showing center, that be comes less and less possible because they just want to hear yes and they are not enough in the loop to make decisions any further than yes or no.

More control

I do not now, nor do I ever mean to imply that it is not hard work to sell your own house. A seller simply does not know what he or she does not know. We have an entirely different book covering just some of the process of selling one's own home. It is not highly technical. It can be simple. But it's not intuitive. We have instructed and helped to oversee hundreds and hundreds of For-Sale-By-Owner transactions.

The Trade-Off is this... More WORK.

You, the seller are the one to get the phone calls, both from agents wishing to show your house, and from people with no agent wishing to view your house. You will get calls with questions, some silly, some just argumentative from agents and the public.

You will have to meet people to gain entrance to your house. You will have to have certain dialogs and conversations with people and you will ultimately have to do some crazy paperwork or respond to some crazy paperwork. All of this can be obtained in advance by using our Graduated Services System or doing more research on the subject, but it is beyond the scope of this book. The point is, there is a lot of stuff to know and a lot of stuff to do, it doesn't just happen. You save a bundle of money, but you have to compute the value of your time and aggravation.

There is also the fact that you will be responsible for your pictures and captions as well as the tent signs. Don't forget the websites, signage, the paperwork (like disclosures for property condition and lead-based paint if applicable) and the very contract itself! So you will earn what you save.

The NEW REAL ESTATE

3 PICTURES

(MONEY SECRET #3 - FOR SELLERS)

PICTURES

In my area, we get twenty pictures in the MLS listing. We don't have to use them all. We really don't have to use any. That would look pretty odd, so you might say the minimum would be one. The one that is called the "primary photo" will be the first one in your photo display and the only shot you see on most websites.

It should be a very attractive, inviting photograph. It should cause the viewer to want to click on it to see more or at least look closer at the listing.

Most people use a straight-on picture of the front of the house, taken from the street at the mailbox as their primary photo. That is usually a pretty safe bet.

DON MARTIN

I have found, over the years, that a photo taken from an angle off to the side, closer to the house and focusing on the front door sometimes to be a friendlier, more inviting shot, but the choice is yours.

Some want fewer than 20. I worked with a gentleman once who wanted only eight pictures of his interior. He said he didn't want everybody to be able to see what kind of stereo he had. Fewer is alright if that is what the customer wants but the potential customer usually wants more.

It doesn't matter whether your house is listed for sale by a Realtor, or if you are selling it yourself with Multiple Listing Service exposure, you need pictures. Even if you are only exposing your house in some local, on-line website, you need pictures. People want to see pictures.

Each type of website probably has a limit on the number of pictures, maybe 1, 5 or in the case of our MLS, 20. Put the maximum number that you can. There is no valid reason to put fewer, even if there are only three rooms in your home, take pictures of the rooms and the exterior from different angles. Put the maximum.

Take the pictures with the best camera you can put your hands on, even if it's a phone. Take them in a horizontal format. Stand as far back as possible to get as much of the room as you can. Wide angle lenses are great, but do the best you can with what you have, and make it better if you ever get the chance and upload the new ones. Look at the picture. If you need to have one portait-style, make sure to turn it upright so that when you upload it, it doesn't look weird lying on its side. If your Realtor is doing the taking, then just look at them as soon as they are uploaded and give your approval. If any are dark, or out of focus, take those over. This is of key importance. It is your home's first impression. And, incidentally, not to insult your intelligence, but get the extra junk, empty glasses, clothes, and "stuff" out of the scene before you snap the pictures. I have seen some before that will make you laugh and cry at the same time.

The next step is to put these pictures in a logical order after uploading. The process of doing this will vary whether you are doing it yourself, or an agent is doing it for his own listing or if an agent is doing it for you as an MLS listing. I won't go into anything that complicated at this point. Just try to have the primary photo of the front followed by the living area, followed by the kitchen and dining areas, followed by the bedrooms and lastly the yard/deck/patio. Order is not a deal-breaker, but out-of-order is sometimes confusing.

Remember these pictures are the link to get someone to come and look at your house, the first step. Until that step is taken, nothing else happens, so these pictures are critically important. The last point I would make is to keep the pictures fresh. If your house stays on the market over a month, take a new primary picture (the front of the house) from a different angle. More pix of the inside will be good, but not as important. You have probably seen before a picture of a house for sale that has snow on the roof, but the actual month is June, so keep them fresh.

All these projects are done differently, depending on your circumstance, so I can't deal with process here but I can individually. if you leave a comment/question. The main idea for you to take away is that your pictures are possibly the most important thing to you at this point. Keep them fresh, and do them right, the way that wouldn't make laugh if you saw them in somebody else's house.

CAPTIONS

On the final step, again, we won't deal with process which is different in various places, but it is adding captions to go along with the pictures. You will have a certain number of spaces for letters. One place I work with, for instance gives us 250 spaces, so you sit and compose a couple of sentences about the picture with letters and spaces that total 250. Don't just say thing like "kitchen," "bedroom"- people can already see that. Say something interesting like "new Sub-Zero refrigerator..." Check to be sure your spelling and word count is RIGHT. Nobody is going to do it for you, and it will look bad if it's wrong. Bullet-lists do not look good after they are uploaded, so make your comments conversational, as though you were talking to the viewer on

The NEW REAL ESTATE
the phone.

A picture is worth a thousand words. Some are only worth nine hundred or so. Pictures start out small when you first see them in the MLS. Then if they interest you, you click on them and they expand. They take you to a larger image.

There you can see more detail. But remember it's more detail of a house that is strange to you. Some cameras even make a difference, but the viewer is only looking at a small portion of the room. There are things about the room you cannot tell no matter how good the detail. (There is Cat 5 cable and double sound insulation behind this wall.)

You, the seller, knows about the house best, so you write them for the picture or for the agent. Don't go over the 250 space mark, or you will lose the end of the sentence.

It makes no difference whether you you are selling your own house and have a flat-rate MLS, or you have listed your house with a full-service Realtor, you still need the detail under the pictures. Tell the agent what you want to do.

One note about using captions that are trite and overworked. You are possibly doing this for the first time, so here's a hint. Try not to use something you have seen or read somewhere else no matter how cute you think it is. It is probably not cute any more to anyone else but you.

On the first, primary photo, don't say "Welcome home to..." That is overdone, to say the least. Also try not to exaggerate. There are not "TONS" of cabinets in your house. Be sensible. Don't insult people's intelligence. Your yard is not like a park to anyone but you. Your home is not "perfect" for any type person or situation, even if it's "good" for it.

VIDEO TOUR

The video tour is fairly recent - may be able to do some yourself but mostly third party. You may have a fairly high-definition video camera or still camera that can take videos. You may have access to or buy, or even download some of the free software available. Even then it will take some considerable time to shoot and edit. You may even do some voice-over, but all this is time consuming, so it really depends on whether that is the highest and best use of your time.

You could also price and then hire a third party to shoot/edit anything from two or three minutes that you could YouTube into your website, the MLS, your emails, and

The NEW REAL ESTATE

social media to a several minute long virtual tour of your property, that can even include aerial views. The longer and more intricate, the more expensive. And whether you are paying the bill, or a listing Realtor is taking the gamble on that investment, the more significant the asking price of your home, the more that risk makes sense.

DON MARTIN

4 TENT SIGNS

(MONEY SECRET #4 - FOR SELLERS)

What are tent signs?

How to make tent signs is probably the most difficult and the most closely guarded secret in real estate today. That of course is a joke. A tent sign is nothing more than a 3x5 card folded long-wise in the middle so that it stands alone.

On the part of the card that can be seen you will print something descriptive about the house. "We have cat 5 cable behind this wall." The house will be able to give its own tour and sell itself.

Whether you are selling your own house For-Sale-By-Owner (FSBO), or whether you have committed to an agent to list

The NEW REAL ESTATE

your house, these little guys are tireless. They will point out EVERYTHING the prospective buyer needs to know, leaving nothing out! Their memory is flawless.

We will get into this are deeper in a future book, but less is more when it comes to the tour of the house, whether it be you or a Realtor. But there are things lookers have to know. You could 1) give them a piece of paper and hope they looked at it at the right time and associate the info with the right room, or you could 2) have tent signs, (or both.)

I have actually had Realtors tell me that they hate the tent signs because signs take control over the prospects. The buyers-to-be start looking for the next sign like an Easter egg hunt, and the house seems to gain control over the lookers instead of the agent having control over them. Ultimately, the house is going to sell the house anyway, not the agent, so that is not a bad thing. So the choice is yours- I think that is good to let the house sell itself.

Of course there are times when tent signs aren't appropriate. You may have small children living in the house. You may not have furniture. Don't be afraid to NOT fold your tent signs, but leave them flat and affix them to an appropriate wall. I have seen tent signs on windows calling attention to a particular view or outdoor feature. Use your imagination!

DON MARTIN

Don't give the "tour..."

The secret trick about tent signs is that the house is going to sell itself. When the right person comes through the door and the magic happens, probably like it did with you, that person will buy that house (if they can, and if you let them.)

No amount of salesmanship is going to sell your house. No Country Club agent, not even you (the house's companion for the last umpteen years) can say or do the exact thing to make somebody buy your house. Only the house can do that.

Actually an agent, even a great one, doesn't know the house very well. They may not yet know their prospects very well. Sometimes the best thing they can do is to back off and not let their presence put extra pressure on the prospects. Prospects like to look at houses by themselves more often than not, so they can just think to themselves, or if a couple, discuss the property without hurting the owner's feelings or involving a stranger into their conversation.

An Owner/seller probably doesn't know the prospects very well. Whether they do or not, the very worst thing they can do is give "the tour" because they invariably end up insulting the looker's intelligence with "this is the kitchen..." The best thing they can do is to add no pressure while a prospect is looking.

I teach a dialog and tip in my regular service that the owner/seller is supposed to sit on the couch in the living room while the prospects look for themselves. It is much easier on the owner/seller, and the prospect receives a much more valuable and productive tour than they otherwise would.

So if the agent backs off and the owner backs off, who tells the prospect that there is cat 5 cable behind that wall? Or about the landscape lighting? Or about the non-skid garage floor?

Who can be non-obtrusive and non-invasive to the mood and still know just the right time to speak, yet have all the appropriate information. Who never leaves out anything, no matter how many times a day they conduct the same tour? Who still has the back-up of the owner on the couch in the front room to answer any questions that may pop up?

Tent signs, that's who.

5 POINTS

(MONEY SECRET - #5 for SELLERS)

What can I do as a seller in terms of being some monetary help to the buyer?

Closing Costs

Well, you can always offer to pay closing costs for seller. A big caveat, though - cap the amount so you know how much you are offering. Specify your maximum.

People ask me all the time how much are closing costs? The answer is, it depends on how you define closing costs. Sometimes a buyer will ask a seller to pay his closing costs. So how do you define closing costs?

Buyers and sellers each have an amount of fees they will pay to the attorney who closes the transaction. Those can be considered closing costs. Sometimes buyers have to pay certain fees associated with their house purchase like mortgage costs, origination fees, etc. Whatever fees you agree to pay will be a help to the buyer, but you really should stipulate a cap on the amount you are willing to pay.

If you have a buyer of your house who is counting pennies before closing, then possibly it is more important to the success of the transaction that you help them with their closing expenses rather than their house note budget. They, or their agent will possibly ask you for BOTH, so this may be the time for the "which is more important?" conversation.

"Boy we are so close and I really like the buyers and I want to see them get this place. In a perfect world, I would surely do both, but I can't, so let me ask you if they had to choose one or the other, which would be more important to them?" Then shut up and wait for an answer. Don't let them have both unless you need to, and only then if it makes sense to you.

What can I do with this $1000?

Let's say I really want to sell faster, so I am going to reduce my sale price. Depending on the total you are asking, $1000 may or may not seem like a a lot. It seems like a lot to me, especially if I have to pay someone that $1000, and that is how you need to look at it. If you take $1000 off the price of your house, it's almost as though you are paying someone that $1000.

Even if it does not appear to be that huge, percentage-wise, there are other things to do with it that will give you more bang for your buck.

If we were to take a house arbitrarily priced at $100,000 and had a buyer who was having to get a mortgage at some arbitrary interest rate, then that $1000 discount might save them 5 or 6 dollars a month on their payment, whereas if you took that same thousand dollars and applied it to what some people call points, or pre-paid interest, it could save them a lot more a month on their house note.

While the amount a point will lower your interest rate will vary, Bob Walters, chief economist at mortgage lender, Quicken Loans in Detroit, says a general rule of thumb is that one point will reduce the rate by ¼ to 3/8 on a 30-year fixed mortgage.

On a $100,000 loan amount for 30 years at 5% the payment would be $536.82 but at an interest rate .25% less the payment would be $521.65, 15 less a month. And at a rate of

The NEW REAL ESTATE
3/8% lower is $513.83, for a savings of $22.98 each month.

But that same $1000 off the sale price drops $536.82 to $531.45, a savings of only $5.37 each month. (Remember none of these payment examples include taxes, insurance or any other fees.)

So if you are working with a buyer who has a tight budget or is very conscious of his payments, this would be a much better use of the money. This does require the seller to explain and educate some buyers and even some agents occasionally.

What if my house has a boo-boo?

If your house has some difficulty that needs attention, some wart that needs removal, nothing that would keep it from being sold, but some nagging item, that if you could make go away, it would be great, then think about this.

People ask me all the time if the should paint this room or that room, and I usually have to tell them no. You will pick the wrong color. People will come to this house with their own palette of colors and you just don't know what those colors are. So here's a thought. Give them a paint allowance.

Instead, you also could offer to give them a check at closing to address the problem. Then the "fix" is up to them. Not only would you probably pick the wrong color, but you also wouldn't do the work as well as they would, or would want you to do, so everyone wins with a check. We're not talking a huge amount here either.

Now if this wart is bigger, and it is an issue and you can't overcome in time to close, you can still give them the money in whatever agreeable amount that works for them, or have the money escrowed, and paid as soon as the work can be completed after closing.

6 BUYER INCENTIVES

(MONEY SECRET #6 - FOR SELLERS)

If you are not in a position to buy your house with cash, you will probably have to get a mortgage to come up with the difference between what you have in cash down payment and purchase price of the house. Several years ago some sellers would finance part of the purchase, thus allowing them to both sell the property and also make a bit of interest on the owner financing.

That is done less these days because of legal issues and many bad experiences, so that is so much less a factor now that this book will not go into that subject on any level. Just know that as a seller, that strategy can help you sell a house that sometimes cannot otherwise be sold, or sell to a buyer who cannot otherwise buy. You as a seller need to weigh the added risk and seek counsel beyond this author.

DON MARTIN

The Refrigerator

Unless you just have to keep it, don't include the refrigerator in the listing even if you intend to leave it. As a point of negotiation then concede them the refrigerator. Or an extra refrigerator in the garage. Just bargain back and forth and one time when it is your turn to drop your price, you can heave a giant, dramatic sigh and throw in the refrigerator as last negotiating chip.

After a certain period of time, when you just want to do some marketing, or if you have heard some remarks about the old stuff, offer new appliances. Be sure to have them picked out, priced, and let everyone know what you're offering, so you know what your cost basis is and the buyer will know what to expect. The best surprise is no surprise. The buyers may want to kick in some of their own bucks and upgrade, but your participation will be clearly defined up front, so don't even bring the upgrade up yourself or they will want it from you. Mention nothing until the contract is finalized.

And one thing I have to tell you right now that will put you out in front of many sellers and, in fact, many Realtors... spell "refrigerator" correctly. In your printed material and in your internet/on-line advertisements, don't just call it a

The NEW REAL ESTATE
"fridge" because you can't spell it. Write it down.

Association Fees

In some communities, the residents kick in a certain amount each month for amenities and services in the immediate area. Sometimes that is a fair amount of money. Sometimes it is just a transition, a culture shock to somebody moving there from the open countryside. Offer to pay their homeowner's dues/fees for six months or a year as an incentive to make it easier to adapt.

Plasma TV

Offer a large flat-panel TV for the bonus room. Technology has progressed more than you may realize. We have gone through technology upgrades past the LCD and LDP projection TVs, past plasma to LED and variations of LED TVs. They are thiner very sharply focused and some even come in 3-D. The prices continue to drop, so you can get a very impressive television for a reasonable amount of money these days. Here again, have it priced, including installation so you will not be surprised and neither will the buyer. Be clear though, (no pun intended) and even have a picture or

DON MARTIN
brochure of it if you can.

7 AGENT INCENTIVES

(MONEY SECRET #7 - FOR SELLERS)

Incentives to an agent

When you come to that point where you feel as though you want to market your home a little bit more aggressively, you may want to offer an incentive or two. You can offer one to a buyer, something that might appeal to someone just surfing the web looking for a home to buy, or you may decide to offer one to the agent who might be bringing a buyer.

With agents, we typically appeal to their dark side. Agents, it seems are in real estate to earn a living. The type-size of the commission number on the listing forms is rather smallish, so if you were to offer a monetary incentive, it is probably better to offer a cash bonus rather that increase their percentage. That gives you the opportunity to stress it more in the Realtor's text area.

DON MARTIN

Agents are not generally excited by other incentives unless they are more significant. Maybe if you run into a sweet deal on a vacation package on some island or on an esoteric German automobile.

Presentation is everything.

When you offer an incentive to the agent, you can be sure to have the word "BONUS" in all caps and in the secret REALTOR REMARKS Section. It's odd, but sometimes a commission seems a lot bigger when it's a certain percentage and a modest cash BONUS (ALL CAPS) than when it's an equivalent amount in percentage only!

It goes without saying a more impressive cash bonus would, of course, just be more impressive! And a fairly late model Porsche would be welcome, too. But ALL CAPS.

The placement of this text is important, too. It needs to be in an area that is seen by the agent but not seen by the prospect. It's not that it's a secret from them, it's just not their concern, and it may even be a distraction.

These days even on a purchase agreement, the commission section has been removed and placed in a separate

The NEW REAL ESTATE document for much the same reasons.

Open a small window of opportunity.

Equally important is the sense of urgency with which you present the bonus. Always make the window of opportunity small- less than two weeks. The last thing you want is an agent taking your bonus for granted, thinking to himself, I've got to show that house someday- there's a bonus on it.

Make it clear that the bonus is for an acceptable offer (as decided by you, but that doesn't have to be stated) by a certain date, and give them two weeks. You can always try again later if it doesn't get the job done this time. And you can raise or lower the bonus.

Another reason for a small window of opportunity is so that you can gauge the success of it. Try one incentive for two weeks, then let the listing rest a week, the try a different one for the next two weeks. Alternate between incentives for buyers and agents and feel free to adjust your asking price down AND UP in conjunction with your different perks. My company give a seller an entire six-month menu on constantly changing perks and incentives so there is never a reason to feel helpless or wonder what to try next.

Never worry about moving your asking price. Yes, you can move up or down. Agents and brokerage offices run update sheets that list four or five items that show up in the inventory since the previous day. One item is a price change. This alerts whoever is watching to a change in the listing price of a house for sale in what ever area they concentrate. A time ago we could make the update sheet in all offices by moving the price a small amount. Nowadays, we have to move the price at least a thousand dollars to qualify to be in that category, but if we can do that from time to time we will increase our chances of being in someones face. Now do that in conjunction with bonus incentives, and you can keep your net figure in the same area but your presence more frequent. Just keep it fresh and frequent.

The best incentive of all.

When it's all said and done, the very best incentive of all for an agent is ease of doing business. I have tried to show houses before that the sellers have made difficult to show- all but impossible to get to show. Always, or at least within reason be willing to let an agent show yor house. Don't impose requirements on the looker's qualifications. Make it easy to show and easy to sell.

8 QR CODES AND WEBSITES

(MONEY SECRET #8 - FOR SELLERS)

What are QR codes?

QR codes are symbols which can be read by a scanner on a cell phone. They usually define an address of a URL to a website. As smart phones and mobile website are growing in popularity, these items are becoming more prevalent as well.

A few years ago the technology was at the point that the seller would put a box by the for sale sign where they kept a supply of fliers about their house. The fliers would have a few pictures and a handful of facts about the house. Hopefully the looker would be interested enough to call and make an appointment to see it for real. At least if there was something about the house that eliminated it as a possibility, then nobody's time got wasted showing them the inside.

Whether it's you or your agent, you can use QR codes on

your sign and even on info fliers if you use them. There are places, sign shops and even websites that will make a QR code for you.

Agents sometimes have them on their sign and sometimes on an accompanying sign swinger. They will direct people, usually prospective buyers who are driving around looking for a house, to their website or to a special website they have created for that house.

The shopper must have a smartphone with a downloaded scanner to have that phone directed to the website, but then they can see pictures of the interior, specs, the price, most all the info available- sometimes from the comfort of their own car if the sign is close to the driveway. And they can view it again from their home or office.

QR codes are being used more and more to get (access to) a lot of information in a small area of a sign, magazine ad, box-top, or business card.

Easy to have your own custom website

Part of the new technology is the ability to generate a website for anything. You can even have a specialized

The NEW REAL ESTATE website for your home.

Addresses to direct your computer to a particular website is called a "URL", a uniform resource locator, which often starts with a "www." with something else in the middle and a ".com" or ".net" on the end. The part in the middle can be long and complicated, or, to make life simpler, the website owner can invest in a "domain name" to substitute. At that point the "url" may be "www.domainname.com".

Taken to its logical next step, one could name a website www.myaddress.com and have information and pictures of your house there. Many Realtors do that now for some of their listings and the individual owner/seller could do that by themselves as well.

In fact, there is an assortment of websites you can use to further your exposure some costing money and some being free. Some, like Craigslist are regional and free, but to maximize your use of them be prepared to spend some time every day posting and renewing so that you can keep up your presence as the tendency is for your ad to get less visible each hour and day.

DON MARTIN

9 SELLER HELP

(MONEY SECRET #9 - FOR BUYERS)

Cash toward points and/or closing costs

If you are not in a position to buy your house with cash, you will probably have to get a mortgage to come up with the difference between what you have in cash down payment and purchase price of the house. Several years ago some sellers would finance part of the purchase, thus allowing them to a) sell the property and b) make a bit of interest on the owner financing.

That is done less these days because of legal issues and many bad experiences, so that is so much less a factor now that this book will not go into that subject on any level. Just know that as a seller that can help you sell a house that sometimes cannot otherwise be sold or to a buyer who cannot otherwise buy. You as a seller need to weigh the added risk and seek counsel beyond this author.

Depending on the type mortgage I am going to get, there may be a maximum that a seller can contribute toward my loan/transaction. Check with your lender to see what the maximum is, and always ask for it from the seller.

Ask for any other perks you might need or want like a years homeowner fee paid or to leave the flat screen, or built-in sound system.

Remember to be sure the cash value does not get in the way of your loan and know that it's best not to ask the seller to include items like a riding lawn mower or other things that are not attached to the property. Such things are called chattel and are best dealt with in a different transaction not as a part of a trans action for the sale of real estate. IE- do a deal, buy it cheap, what ever helps you, just not in the house contract.

Ask for the moon - Yes, that's right. Anything you see, you specify in the offer. I have seen sellers take their mailbox, spring bulbs, and ornate half-bath mirror frames. Don't say "hey- it was attached! They shouldn't have taken that!" If you even THINK you might whine about it when it's gone before you actually move in, specify in the offer!

In fact list stuff you don't even care about. Ask for it. It looks better on you every time you concede something. If there is a basement, specify that it be cleaned out. If there is a crawl space, specify that it be cleaned out. If there's an attic- well you know... Don't have a bunch of projects waiting for you to address in your new home.

You would be foolish not to have a home inspection and to subsequently ask for everything on the inspector's punch list to be repaired before you sign off and remove your contingency for an acceptable inspection.

The Rest of the Cast

The rest of the cast you have assembled, besides your trusted **Realtor**, will be a **Closing attorney**, a **Lender,** and a **home inspector**.

Your closing attorney ideally would be someone you have used previously and with whom you are comfortable. Don't be afraid to interview a couple at least by phone. I say by phone, because typically attorneys stay busy and one of their unspoken goals in business is to stay booked so that they have they little (if only visible) free time. So respect that and talk to them for a minute or two on the phone.

You want to feel comfortable talking with them. That quickly became one of my most important yardsticks when I was early into the business. Closing companies use very similar software, one to the next so their accuracy is almost always good and their fees are competitive, so they are quite similar, but the big difference is the personality.

I have had customers close before (and before I knew) with someone who seemed gruff and almost unwilling to answer their questions or take the needed time to explain things. This, in the end, made me look bad, and during the closing, made me feel uncomfortable. And I wasn't even the buyer or seller!

So decide on someone you feel good about talking to and seem to at least up front be willing to answer your questions. They will not make a lot of money off of you by yourself, but you want them to make you feel as though they are.

Fee-wise, as I said they are all pretty similar. You may have an Uncle Harry who is an attorney and will close your transaction for seventy five cents, but that is the exception, worth consideration but not worth dealing with here.

The lender could be your personal bank or personal credit union, a new-to-you bank, credit union or mortgage company, or a mortgage broker who works with a couple or more lenders to get you a good rate but not restricted to one mortgage company.

Here again talk to a few and pick one who can not only give you the best interest rates, but one who is agreeable to deal with and talk to. You will be sharing a lot of personal information here, so make sure you are comfortable with them. Here again, rates will probably competitive, but one may have a service that works better for you. Just be sure he/she seems competent and friendly/agreeable.

And lastly, find a home inspector. Here it doesn't matter whether on not he is agreeable. In fact, picky and coarse is not bad here. You will probably pick one that one of your friends has used and liked, or one who gives you a book with the inspection. Just make sure he/she can come to your house within a day or two and or typically make you wait a week or so.

10 AGENT HELP

(MONEY SECRET #10 - FOR BUYERS)

Rebate part of commission

Look for a Realtor who is willing to share part of their commission with you in the form of a rebate. Different states have different laws about this, but most states are very serious about not letting an agent give a buyer a sack of cash. Banks and the Federal government don't like it either.

Usually you can't get cash as a part of a real estate transaction unless you are licensed. States are very strict. If an agent buys you a cup of coffee, don't even CALL it commission.

Most of the time a buyer can receive a non-monetary gift for doing business as long as the details and requirements are spelled out in advance, and everyone from the agent to his broker to the buyer knows the actual incentive and what it takes to earn it. It's gonna vary from state to state, so if you do have any questions, you can always call your state real estate commission to ask them.

But if you are willing to do some of the work finding your new house, then some buyers feel as though they would rather not call the agent whose name is on the sign and let them get twice the commission. They feel it's better that a buyer work with a non-greedy buyer's agent who would prefer get a percentage of a commission from out of the blue than none at all.

This sharing can take the form of gift cards or housewarming gifts. You can read more about this in my other book about my Graduated Real Estate Services. For now, just think outside the old proverbial. And find an agent who does, too.

Send you search results

Now the way you earn part of that reward is to do part of the work. You do what you love. And what you're gonna do any way. Surf the web. Go to REALTRACS or somewhere and look at the houses for sale. Go to open houses on the weekend. If you see some that are on the web that you like, but are not open, then call the agent with whom you have the arrangement and get them to gain entrance for you.

Sometimes Realtors work a deal like this on a sliding scale where the fewer houses they have to show you, the more rebate you get, so be careful. Its easy to get caught up and enjoy looking at a LOT of houses. And that defeats the purpose for the Realtor.

Your Realtor can program a search in the MLS system that will look for what you want and automatically send you an email when something like that is put on the market. You drive by to be sure you like it, and the call your agent and get in. Procrastination here will only bring problems, so don't wait until the weekend if it's not absolutely necessary.

You hit open houses

See if your town published an Open house preview on Friday or Saturday, and make an itinerary. Look at RealTracs.com. Go to the Open Houses section and specify the neighborhood you like. Get your itinerary there. Just know that the hours of 2 'til 4 Sunday go by quickly, and you can hit twice as many with a plan than without one.

Make notes, and even snap a couple of pictures in each house you tour. They will run together very soon if you don't.

Call to gain entry

Obviously, I am doing the looking on line, at open houses, and driving by computer generated possibilities, and when one turns up I like I am going to get my agent to compose and submit our offer.

He or she already has some of the details of the offer written out so it should not be too much trouble for the agent.

This is probably a good time to point out that, in addition to the other aspects of this Realtor, it would be good if he were appropriately set up with HUD to be able to make bids for you on some foreclosed properties on which you can make a fair amount of money if you are inclined, able, or have people who are able to fix them up to a condition to be rented or resold.

The NEW REAL ESTATE
CONCLUSION

OK, perhaps some of this stuff you have heard before, but most you have not even thought about. I will be busy soon finishing companion books, continuing your education and helping to make you feel good about spending the money to buy this book, and taking the time to read it.

These ideas in their own ways, were about finance, sales and representation in the transaction of buying or selling a house or property. Trying any one or more of the concepts will bring you immediate results. The more you study and practice any of these areas, the more valuable they can become to you as you get more proficient at them. Think of this as a general education. If one in particular intrigues you, you could do graduate work in that area, and it would become even more valuable to you. But if you stop right here and put these into use, they will be worth many thousands of dollars to you.

DON MARTIN
ABOUT THE AUTHOR

Don Martin

Martin Properties

Graduated Services Real Estate

(615) 973-8970

My name is Don Martin, author, speaker, and Broker/Owner of Martin Properties. Since there is a possibility you may hire me someday, please consider this a sort of resume, if you will.

- Licensed, full-time real estate since 1984, almost thirty years. (GOOGLE us- we're not obscure, new-comers to this business.)
- Vanderbilt University and Peabody Demonstration School (University School)
- Christ Church on Old Hickory Blvd over twenty five years.
- Married over thirty five years.
- HUD certified as Buyer's Agent
- You probably won't find me at a retreat trying to get in touch with myself. I'd rather get in touch with you.
- Fairly stable. I keep my promises. I stay in touch. I

The NEW REAL ESTATE

return calls.
- My work carries a MONEY-BACK GUARANTEE!
- A portion of the proceeds go to benefit Safe Haven Family Shelter.
- I treat your business as the blessing that it is to me.
- I save people A LOT of MONEY!

Don is available to speak to your group or workshop. Please call at (615)973-8970 & join at sites below.

www.MartinPropertiesOnline.com

www.FSBO-GUY.com

www.theReasonableRealtor.com

martindo@realtracs.com

SOME TESTIMONIALS

"I highly recommend working with Martin Properties to sell your house if you are considering for sale by owner (FSBO). I wanted to do FSBO to save money, but I was unsure of the process. I found out about Martin Properties when I was searching for our new house and saw a property on his website. Don made the process so easy, telling us what steps we needed to do -- and what not to do -- and I could call him whenever I had a question, so we were never alone during the process. Within 7 days of Don listing our house on MLS, we had 3 offers! Don gave me advice on how to handle multiple offers, and within a couple of days we accepted the

DON MARTIN

best offer, which matched our goal of what we wanted to get out of the sale. All I had to do was show the house and coordinate details with the buyer's realtor (we chose to pay a buyer's agent commission) and Don as needed. It was so worth the modest fee we payed to Martin Properties! We're even buying our new house from one of his clients!"
- Pam Hull, Nashville, August 2013

"Don presented with a very warm and professional manner. He spoke with good knowledge of the subject and answered my questions with patience. He never seemed to be in a hurry but allowed me time to understand the paperwork, which I always need in a situation. I would highly recommend him to work with clients and be helpful. It was good and a very positive experience."
- Frances C. (Worked with Don Martin in 2012 in Nashville, TN)

"Our home buying experience was an exciting one! Don was great!! He was always there when my husband and I needed his time or input regarding us buying a home. He never rushed us but had a great deal of patience and information to share. He was with us every step of the way, and we are very thankful and grateful that he was apart of this experience!!!!"
- Eustalyn (Bought a home with Don Martin in 2012 in Nashville, TN)

The NEW REAL ESTATE

"**You are number ONE! Very understanding and professional.** Thanks for everything!"

Mrs. Elizabeth Harper
Brentwood, TN

THANK YOU to Don Martin and Martin Properties for providing this innovative and invaluable service. Don's years of experience and expertise in real estate and simple straight-forward approach is the perfect formula for anyone considering selling by owner. Exactly what we were looking for.

M. Dailey

Thanks Don for helping us sell our home so quickly. Listing on the MLS certainly made a difference in the number of calls we received to see the house and we received 3 offers after you listed it. We accepted the 3rd full priced contract within a month of the listing. Thanks so much for all of your help and assistance. You can be sure that we'll use you again next time.

DON MARTIN

Bobby and Gayle Williams

"Having owned a marketing and communications firm for over 13 years, I have a high appreciation for excellent customer service and measurable results. I'm pleased to share that my experience with Don Martin has hit **top scores on both marks**.

Don's **high level of professionalism and straight shooting answers** provided us with strategic insight and the foundation we needed to handle the sale of our home by ourselves. Don was more than willing to answer all of our questions and help in any way he could. I highly recommend Don Martin for your MLS listing needs should you choose to sell your home 'by owner'."

Mike   Keil
President
The Resource Agency

June 8, 2008

I could not have had a better experience and better results with Don Martin and Martin Properties. Don made it easy to get started with his no-nonsense listing agreement and the sample forms he gave me to assist in the process. I took all the calls and did all the showings and all the negotiations. My closing attorney took it the rest of the way with the details of the payoff and HUD-1 Buyers/Sellers settlement sheet. And to top it all off I PAID NO SELLER, OR BUYER AGENT COMMISSIONS AT ALL!!! ZIP, ZILCH, NADA, NOT A DIME!!!! That was a total SAVINGS OF MORE THAN $11,000.00!! Even in a slumping housing market (2007-2008) and less than stellar economy my FSBO listing through Don Martin did the trick. Additionally, doing my own market research, I priced my house for $10,000 more than the agents I visited with had told me they would price it at--and I got it!!! Statistically, 83 percent of buyers find their house on the internet. Now that I've done this myself, I really do wonder what a conventional agent does for the outrageous commissions they are asking. The Martin Properties way works!

Thanks Don,

Jim Piekarski

"**As a former Realtor I heartily recommend Don's service.** Don made it possible for our home to be posted in the MLS for a minimal amount of money. As a result our home sold in less than a month and we saved $$$!!! He was great to work with, **always ready to help in any way possible.** We

DON MARTIN
would not hesitate a minute to call him again."

Ray & Jan Rains

"From the moment that I met Don I knew that this program would work for me. We had spent a couple of weeks preparing our house to sell. Touching up paint, removing all of the clutter, just making it a showplace for potential buyers. Taking the time to prepare you home for selling and not for living will make your home more desirable for potential buyers, so make sure you take the time to do those things.

I tried the old fashioned FSBO and had a couple of Open Houses, but had no offers or even any serious prospects. After a couple of weeks of this I decided to call Don and get my house listed on the MLS, Realtracs, and realtor.com, and **within 2 weeks I had a solid contract from a qualified buyer**, making it possible for us to buy the house that we had been hoping to buy.

If you are thinking at all about selling your home please give Don a call. **It is a phone call that will save you thousands!!!!!**

Thanks for everything Don!!!"

The NEW REAL ESTATE

Robert Bedenbaugh

Yes, it sold in a week w/2 contracts!! Should have listed it for more $$$;-)

Lynne, Franklin (December 2007)

"Thanks for your service. It was a very fast process. Two weeks on the MLS and I had a contract with a full price offer. Two weeks after signing the contract I closed saving thousands in realtor commission fees. I will definitely use your service the next time I sell."

Mark Sherrell

"He makes us feel like we're his only customers. I mean, I know we're not, but we feel that way... Thanks!"

DON MARTIN

We contacted Don after business hours on a Monday night. He met with us Tuesday morning to complete the paperwork for listing our house. It was on line Tuesday night and by that Thursday we had a full price offer. Don was available for questions regarding the sales contract for our home and provided thoughtful and insightful advice. We came to an agreement with the sellers by Friday and had a binding contract before our first open house. SOLD IN 48 HOURS AT FULL ASKING PRICE!!! We couldn't be more pleased.

Erin and Jason Parker

"I remember your kindness and help to us in our transition. Thank you."

Billy Sprague, Music Ministry

Franklin, now Colorado

The NEW REAL ESTATE

New in the business of real estate investing, we turned to Don to help us list our first rehab house. Don not only listed our property, he showed the house for us while we were out of town, and gave us very valuable guidance when we got an offer. Don was instrumental in us being able to sell our house for full asking price. Thanks Don.

Lee & Pamela Nelson

Red Square Properties

Dr. Martin,

"Our neighbors just recently listed their house through you as a FSBO and it **sold for the asking price in 5 days after being on the market without you for 3 months.** My wife and I are getting ready to put our townhouse on the market around the beginning of September.

Thank you in advance for your assistance."

"We had two homes to sell and wanted to save the extra % of the sale price and needed to get the MLS exposure. Don was recommended and within a few days he met with us and outlined the process. We were impressed and immediately made the decision to go with him. As soon as we got the sign in the yard and the posting on MLS we had calls to show the house. **The first house sold in five days and the second home sold in two.** Don used the MLS and his web site to give us the exposure we needed, which included pictures of the house. He also went above and beyond to help answer contract questions. It was important for us to have a local contact and someone we could rely on. **Martin Properties was exactly what we were looking for and the experience exceeded our expectations."**

Kevin and Cindi Applegate

"I used to sell real estate in California, and I saw your ad in the Christian Classifieds. I just want to ask you one question. **Is this legal?**"

-Anonymous lady telephone caller, Mar 3, 2007

<u>Don,</u>
<u>Thank you very much for your assistance. Your price for your service was well worth it. I paid only one percent to</u>

The NEW REAL ESTATE

the realtor plus my cost for your service which allowed me to save about $6,000 in commissions over having gone the typical route of listing with a realtor. That is a GRANDIOUS savings in my book. It also made it so much easier with the MLS lock on the door. It saved me even more time not having to run to the condo all the time for a showing.
Thanks again and you are already being referred by me to others.

Max Sanders
A Magical Wish
www.amagicalwish.com

"Martin Properties allowed me to obtain an MLS listing at a small fee in order to reach more potential buyers for my "For Sale by Owner" home in the West End area. Don was always available by phone or email to answer any questions and help as much or as little as desired during the process.

I would recommend Martin Properties to list your FSBO home on the MLS to anyone who wants to save thousands of dollars on Realtor commissions - it is well worth the small amount of extra effort required on the part of the owner. **This service is long-overdue!** Thanks, again Don!"

Constance Sinclair

Nashville, TN

DON MARTIN

"Doc Martin,

We sure appreciate the job you did. You were a pleasure to work with. We will definitely be recommending you to others!"

"Hi Don:

We are very pleased with the results of listing our home for sale using your reduced fee program. **We averaged about 6 showings per week**" ... "The interesting part is that the buyers had been on a mission trip for several months in Bolivia and had been <u>tracking our home by internet</u> until they returned home. **<u>Very satisfied with the service</u>**--thank you again."

Bob & Candace
Franklin, TN

"**I have used Martin Properties personally** to help me and my wife sell our home as well as purchase a new one. **I also refer my clients** that do not have a Realtor because I know they will give my clients the same attention they gave me when I needed the help. **I would recommend anyone** that is looking to purchase or sell a home to consider the personal attention you will get when using Martin Properties."

Lehman Hailey, Jr
President Evergreen Mortgage

"**I recommend Martin Properties**. As a former customer, I found their service and performance to be exemplary.

We sold our house for the amount we wanted, in less than twenty-four hours, then found our current home at an incredible price. Everything about the deal was smooth and simple, with every twist and turn navigated with ease.

We have been living in our current home for about six years and could not be more satisfied, but should we ever want or need to relocate, the first call goes to Martin Properties."

Kirby W. Allen
Brentwood, TN

DON MARTIN

"Cindy and I would like to thank you for your help in selling our home and for the purchasing of our new home. **You showed incredible poise** keeping all parties calm when the buyers for our home became difficult. In the end we sold high and bought low. **Who could ask for more?"**

Richard and Cindy Furman
Southwest Lawns

"My compliments on the **professionalism, knowledge and patience** that you provided while representing me in both the sale of my former home and the purchase of my new home. I would unequivocally **recommend you to anyone** needing professional real estate representation."

Michael Smith
Former treasurer Harpeth Trace Homeowners Association

"Thanks for all your help. **This was a great experience for me.** Please feel free to refer anyone in the future to me for a

The NEW REAL ESTATE referral on your service."

Alex Simpson

Fredericksburg - Brentwood, TN

"I look forward to a continued relationship with you and your company. We will be looking for a new project (house)..."

Lynne Weeks

Smyrna, TN

"Thanks for all your help!"

Carless Dance

Mt. Juliet, TN

"Thanks again for representing us! I am so glad that you

called me and that we decided to use you as our agent. You literally saved us thousands of dollars! I wish you the best of luck and truly hope that you succeed in this venture. I don't know how you can't! I will recommend you to anyone looking to sell their home.

Thanks again!"

Harrison Hudnall

"We had attempted to sell our home on our own by using directional signs and listing it in the Tennessean. After several weeks, we had no offers and no one really interested. Don Martin approached us about listing our home on the MLS while still being able to sell it by owner. Within a couple of weeks we had several interested lookers and by the third week we not only had one offer but two with a third one waiting to see if the sale would go through. I would **highly recommend the service Don provides**. We had our house listed in the MLS for a reasonable fee and <u>**saved thousands on real estate fees**</u>. We will definitely use this service again if selling a property and **would encourage anybody else to do so as well.**"

Jim and Elizabeth Wash,

Brentwood, TN

The NEW REAL ESTATE

"Thank you for all your help on the sell of our condo. We **listed it on a Wednesday, and we had a signed contract by Monday.** I do appreciate your help. We could not have done it without you.

Thank you,"

Scott Cone

Nashville Mortgage Company, LLC

November 6, 2005

Dear Don,

We have to write and thank you for helping us quickly sell our home this year. We tried Marketing the house ourselves but it soon became obvious that most of the "lookers' were exactly that- "lookers". We had one serious homebuyer but he kept dragging his feet about the actual offer to buy. That is when we decided to call you. After meeting you and totally understanding your unique service, we made the decision to let you help us. That evening the information regarding our home was on the Internet! We found it hard to believe when **the next morning brought a qualified buyer to our home, which resulted in an offer to buy our home at our asking price that afternoon!** We feel so fortunate in finding you and want to thank you as well as compliment you on your professional and very efficient service. Best of luck in the future.

Bob and Claudette Walsh

Don,

Just a brief note of thanks for your help in selling my home. Your service is **very valuable** for anyone who is in the position to market and show their home on their own. Getting access to the MLS and Realtor.com is invaluable. I appreciate your willingness to meet with inspectors, etc. when I was out of town to ensure the process continued forward in a timely manner.

Regards,
Kim G.

Hi Don, **I have about 3 people who will be calling you** within the next few months to use your services. thanks.

Jeana

The NEW REAL ESTATE

"We sold our house with Martin Properties. **It was really pretty effortless.** Don Martin explained the program, took some photos, got us on the MLS and the next thing we knew agents started calling to set appointments. **We had an accepted offer in 48 hours.** There's just no need to pay an agent 1-3% of the value of your home to list your property when it's just as easy to go with Martin Properties at a **fraction of the cost.**"

Dave Gallagher

The sale went **fast, cheap and smoothly.**

Mike Dioguardi
Robin Hill Rd.

We thank you for **giving us the courage...**

Ann Olsen

"I want to thank you for all your help and consideration in

the sale of our Robin Hill Road property in West Meade. Once we finished the remodel on this house, listed it with your company and appeared in Multiple Listing, **I was inundated with phone calls**. On the first weekend we had so many appointments for Realtors to show the house that it appeared to be an open house. The lock box made that task very easy for us. **By Sunday we had 2 contracts both as over bids**. The following week I was asked if we could accept another. **With the substantial savings on commissions our deal was most gratifying.**

<u>We will definitely use your service again</u>."

Sincerely,

Michael J. Dioguardi
James Michael Halloran

"Martin Properties is the **perfect solution** for the do-it yourself with the MLS exposure. Mr. Martin was **always approachable and willing to answer questions**. I was able to sell a difficult property fairly quickly. I was very **pleased with the service and plan to use this formula again in the future. Thank you....**"

Thank you Don for the help..

Stephan Francois

The NEW REAL ESTATE

"Thank you for all your help. Without your service I don't know that we would have ever sold. **FYI we sold on our 46th showing.** This is a remarkable number because we took a week off and didn't show the house when we went out of town and **had five agents call to setup a showing on the day we sold.** So our number of showing would have been around 55 in just over six weeks. Wow!."

Jason Obester
Spring Hill

www.ingramcontent.com/pod-product-compliance
Lightning Source LLC
Chambersburg PA
CBHW071802200526
45167CB00017B/1045